CHANITA R. RAMSEY

Unchained: The Awakening of the Empath's Soul Workbook

First published by Inspired by Love & Grace Publishing 2026

First edition

ISBN: 978-1-970671-11-7

This book was professionally typeset on Reedsy.
Find out more at reedsy.com

Dedication

To every woman who has poured out her heart only to feel empty...
To every empath who has been silenced, manipulated, or broken ...
To every soul walking through the fire of betrayal, pain, and isolation—
this workbook is for you.
May these pages give you the clarity you've longed for,
the courage you didn't know you had,
and the strength to rise into your awakening.
You are not alone.
You are not forgotten.

Contents

Acknowledgments

First and foremost, I thank God for His unfailing love, His steady guidance, and His patient hand upon my life. Every season of brokenness was met with His presence, every silent moment was filled with His strength, and every victory was born from His grace.

To the women who shared their stories with honesty and vulnerability—your courage fuels this ministry. Your voices, your tears, and your truth have become the heartbeat of this work.

To my family, my children, and every supporter who has stood beside me—thank you for reminding me of the power of love, faith, and unwavering support. Your belief in me has been a constant source of strength.

And to every empath who turns the pages of this workbook:

May you know—deeply and unapologetically—that your sensitivity is not a flaw but a divine gift.

Your heart is sacred.

Your light is needed.

Your soul is equipped to soar far beyond the pain that tried to silence you.

Thank you for trusting me with your healing journey.

May this be the beginning of your awakening, your restoration, and your freedom.

Introduction – Using This Workbook

This workbook has one purpose: **your awakening**.

These pages were created to lead you through a journey of truth-telling, emotional healing, spiritual alignment, and personal transformation. Whether you walk this path alone or with others, this workbook will challenge you, stretch you, and strengthen you.

You may use this workbook **on its own**, or alongside
Unchained: The Awakening of the Empath's Soul.

Either way, you are about to enter a journey that will demand honesty, courage, and consistency.

This is not passive reading.

This is intentional, soul-level work.

How to Walk This 12-Week Journey

Let me be absolutely clear: **this is not a cute devotional. This is spiritual rehab.**

There will be days when you want to close this book and pretend you never started.

Those days matter the most.

Breakthrough happens when you refuse to run from hard truth.

- Some days you will feel exposed.
- Some days you will feel angry.
- Some days you will feel deeply seen and finally understood.

Keep going.

Transformation does not come to the comfortable—it comes to the committed.

This journey is not for the faint of heart. It is for the woman who is **done living chained.**

How to Use Each Week

Every week has a **theme** and a **Scripture of the Week** to anchor your mind and spirit.

Every day has **specific work**—no guessing, no drifting, no skimming.

You will:

- **Read**
- **Reflect**
- **Write**
- **Confront**
- **Confess**
- **Act**

You may not always "feel" like doing it.

Do it anyway.

Growth rarely feels good in the moment, but it always produces fruit.

How to Use This Workbook

Individually

Take your time. Reflect honestly. Write freely. Let your truth come out without censoring yourself. Healing requires transparency, and transparency requires courage.

In Groups

Use the discussion prompts to share safely, build trust, support each other, and discover strength through community.

Each module includes:

- **Chapter Summary** – The emotional and spiritual insights for that week.
- **Reflection Questions** – Prompts to help you uncover patterns, pain points, and truths.
- **Exercises** – Journaling assignments and transformational writing practices.
- **Group Discussion Prompts** – Optional, but powerful for group healing.
- **Action Steps** – Practical movement toward emotional clarity and healthy boundaries.
- **Affirmations / Reflection Pages** – Declarations to help you rewire your mindset and rise into your identity.

A Final Word Before You Begin

This journey will not just change how you think—it will change how you show up, how you love, how you see yourself, and how you allow yourself to be loved.

Some pages will feel like mirrors.

Some will feel like medicine.

Some will feel like war.

All will feel like truth.

You are ready because you are here.

Now breathe deeply.

Open your heart.

And begin your awakening.

WEEK 1 — AWAKENING TO THE HUNGER

Your Need Is Not a Curse — It's a Clue.

Anchor Scripture of the Week

Psalm 34:18 (NIV)

"The Lord is close to the brokenhearted and saves those who are crushed in spirit."

This scripture grounds the entire week. Hunger is a form of spiritual crushing—God is closest there.

Personal Story of the Week — "The Night My Hunger Spoke Louder Than My Hope"

There was a night when I sat alone in my car after another argument with someone I loved far more than he ever had the capacity to love me back. I had poured into him endlessly—fixing, forgiving, waiting, hoping. I kept telling myself, *"If I just love him better, he will finally choose me the way I choose him."*

But that night changed everything.

He walked away mid-conversation again, leaving me sitting on the edge of the bed holding words he did not care enough to stay and hear. I drove off after he left, heart pounding, tears falling faster than I could wipe them.

I parked in an empty lot and held the steering wheel until my hands ached. Through trembling breaths I whispered:

"Why do I always end up here? Why am I never enough?"

The answer didn't come from God immediately—

it came from my hunger.

My hunger said:

"Because you are trying to feed parts of your soul with people who don't have the capacity to nourish you."

In that moment, I realized I wasn't chasing him.

I was chasing the feeling of being chosen.

Of being seen.

Of being worth fighting for.

My hunger made me believe breadcrumbs were a feast.

That night, sitting alone in that car, I finally saw it:

My hunger was not my shame.

My hunger was my **signal**—a divine alarm calling me out of emotional starvation and into awakening.

And this week, that same awakening begins for you.

Weekly Focus

This week you will confront the deep emotional hunger that has drawn you into unhealthy patterns, relationships, and cycles. Instead of judging it, you will learn to understand it, name it, and listen to what it has been trying to reveal about you.

Many empaths spend years giving, serving, loving, and pouring without ever asking a crucial question:

"What am I hoping to receive?"

The truth is simple and transformative:

Your hunger is not your enemy.

Your hunger is your messenger.

Optional Reading (Companion Book)

Unchained: The Awakening of the Empath's Soul — Introduction + "The Hunger" themes.

Key Truth of the Week

The hunger that embarrassed you is not a flaw.

It is a signal that you were meant for more than crumbs.

This hunger is not a weakness—it is a divine alarm, awakening you to the places where you have settled for less, tolerated too much, or accepted emotional leftovers in the name of love.

By the End of Week 1, You Will:

- Identify where you have over-given and under-received.
- Name what you were truly craving beneath each relationship.
- Begin to see your hunger as a guide rather than a burden.
- Start releasing shame connected to your emotional needs.

Part One – The Hunger

Exploring the empath's craving for love, attention, and affirmation.

Full Summary

Many empaths carry a deep, unspoken hunger for love, affirmation, safety, belonging, and emotional connection. This hunger is often rooted in childhood wounds, unmet needs, or seasons of feeling unseen, unheard, or undervalued. Because of this, empaths frequently overextend themselves—giving far more than they have, hoping that love will heal or transform another person.

In the introduction of the companion book, Igo into depth sharing my emotional journey—loving deeply while rarely feeling fully received. What felt like weakness was actually God's refining tool. The hunger wasn't designed to break me—it was designed to awaken me.

The breaking you experienced was not destruction.

It was revelation.

It exposed what needed healing.

It revealed what needed boundaries.

It awakened the part of you that has been silent too long.

Your hunger is not a curse.

It is a compass.

Key Takeaway

The chains that tried to break you are also the tools that awaken your soul.

Your hunger is not a flaw—it is guidance toward your growth, strength, and divine purpose.

Reflection Questions for Week 1

Write freely and honestly. Give each answer at least one thoughtful paragraph.

1. Recall a time when you gave too much of yourself emotionally. What were you hoping to receive in return?
2. How have moments of feeling unseen or unappreciated shaped the way you see yourself?
3. In what ways can your emotional hunger guide you toward truth instead of pulling you into pain?
4. What do you feel God—or your higher self—is using this hunger to teach you?

Core Exercise 1 – Identifying the Hunger

Choose three to five situations from your past or present where you:

- Over-gave
- Over-invested
- Over-loved
- Over-accommodated

For each situation, write:

- What relationship or situation it was
- What you were craving (love, safety, attention, security, being chosen, being needed, being seen)
- How that hunger influenced your behavior
- How it affected your emotional, mental, or spiritual well-being
- What you want to do differently going forward

Do not soften the truth.

Honesty heals what hiding harms.

Core Exercise 2 – Releasing the Weight

Letter of Honesty to God or Your Higher Self

Begin with this prompt:

"God, I release my burden to You. I admit that I have chased love, attention, and affirmation in places that starved me. I trusted people who could not hold my heart. I gave until I was empty. I am tired of pretending I'm fine. Show me what this hunger is really trying to teach me..."

Write until you feel empty...

then breathe until you feel light.

Let your tears speak if they must.

They are part of the release.

Group Discussion Prompts (Optional)

Use these only if working through the workbook with others:

- Share a moment when empathy caused you to overgive and what it cost you.
- Discuss how understanding the purpose behind the pain shifts your perspective.
- Explore ways your group can strengthen emotional boundaries while still loving openly.

Action Step – This Week

Choose one person, situation, or role in your life where you feel overextended. This week:

- Set one boundary
- Take one step back
- Say one honest "no"
- Honor one emotional limit

At week's end, journal:
"How did honoring my limits affect my mood, peace, and energy?"
Your body and spirit will tell the truth before your mind does.

Weekly Declaration

Speak this aloud daily:
"I am awakening.
My hunger is not shameful—it is holy information.
I am worthy of real love, not emotional scraps."

Daily Regimen for Week 1

Day 1 – Sit With the Scripture and the Hunger

- Read your Scripture of the Week slowly, at least three times.
- Write every word or phrase that stands out.
- Finish this sentence:
- **"If I'm honest, what I'm really hungry for in this season is...**"

Day 2 – First Truths, First Tears

- Re-read the Week 1 summary.
- Write about a time you gave too much and ended up empty.
- List three things you wish you had done differently—not to shame yourself, but to awaken yourself.

Day 3 – Reflection Questions, No Hiding

- Answer each reflection question in depth.
- After each answer, write:
- "The truth I didn't want to admit here is..."

Day 4 – The Letter You've Avoided

Write your Letter of Honesty in full.
Let yourself break open on the page.
God heals what you reveal.

Day 5 – One Boundary in Real Life

- Pick one situation where you overextend.
- Set one boundary today.
- Tonight, journal:

- "This is what it felt like to protect my heart today..."

Day 6 – What the Hunger Has Cost You

Write:

"Because I ignored my hunger, I paid the price in these ways..."

Then write:

"I refuse to keep paying this price for counterfeit love."

Day 7 – Weekly Review, Prayer, and Declaration

- Review everything you wrote this week.
- Pray for courage to honor your hunger without shame.
- Declare boldly:
- "I am awakening. My soul is strong, my heart is sacred, and I am stepping into freedom one moment at a time."

WEEK 2 — DETOXING FROM THE DRUG OF AFFIRMATION

No More Being High on Being Chosen

Anchor Scripture of the Week

Galatians 1:10 (NIV)

"Am I now trying to win the approval of human beings, or of God? ... If I were still trying to please people, I would not be a servant of Christ."

Why this scripture:

This week is all about the bondage of approval and the addictive "high" of being chosen. Galatians 1:10 pierces straight through the illusion:

You cannot serve the approval of people and also walk in the freedom God ordained for you.

Personal Story of the Week —"The Compliment That Became a Chain"

I remember the exact moment the "drug of affirmation" first hooked its claws into me. It wasn't romantic, it wasn't intimate—it was simple, almost innocent. He said six words I didn't know I'd been starving for:

"You make me feel understood and seen."

Those words wrapped around my heart so tightly that I didn't realize they were forming a leash.

At first, it felt good—no, it felt intoxicating.

Someone admired my empathy.

Someone praised my presence.

Someone noticed what others overlooked.

And because my soul had been neglected for so long, that tiny dose of affirmation felt like oxygen.

But I didn't notice how quickly I became dependent on it.

I started answering calls I didn't want to take.

I listened to stories that drained me dry.

I rearranged my life to meet his needs.

I ignored my own exhaustion because I couldn't bear the thought of losing the only place where I felt "seen."

It didn't matter that he was inconsistent.

It didn't matter that he rarely reciprocated.

It didn't matter that something always felt "off."

I was chasing the high of being chosen.

One day, after pouring out more of myself than I had to give, I realized something:

His praise felt like water, but it was pulling me toward drowning.

Every compliment cost me a boundary.

Every moment of being "seen" required me to disappear a little more.

And when he finally withdrew the affirmation I had become addicted to, I discovered something painful:

It wasn't him I was grieving—

I was grieving the version of myself I sacrificed to keep his praise flowing.

That day, something shifted in me.

I heard God whisper:

"What you crave from them, you were meant to receive from Me."

And now, this week, you will confront the exact same truth.

This is where detox begins.

Weekly Focus

This week you will uncover the emotional "addiction" that forms when praise, validation, and attention become your drug of choice. You will identify the first moments in life when you felt unseen, the patterns that formed because of it, and the ways affirmation has shaped your decisions—even your relationships.

This is not about shame.

This is about clarity.

The question guiding this week is simple:

"What am I trying to prove when I want to be praised?"

Optional Reading (Companion Book)

Unchained: The Awakening of the Empath's Soul — Chapter 1: The Drug of Affirmation

Key Truth of the Week

The praise that thrilled you was never proof of your worth—only proof of your hunger.

By the End of Week 2, You Will:

- Identify where affirmation has controlled you.
- Recognize how praise created blind spots and emotional bonds.
- Understand the "high" you chased and what wound it fed
- Begin detaching your identity from people's approval.

Part Two – The Drug of Affirmation

Why Being "Chosen" Felt Like Oxygen

Full Summary

Many empaths fall into cycles of being emotionally overextended because affirmation feels like nourishment. When someone offers praise, admiration, or "love-bombing," it awakens deeply rooted needs inside the empath—needs for validation, belonging, attention, connection, and being chosen.

This "drug of affirmation" always begins beautifully.

It feels spiritual.

It feels romantic.

It feels like destiny.

But it's not destiny—it's dopamine.

And once the empath is hooked, the pattern begins:

They give more.

They tolerate more.

They silence themselves more.

They hope harder.

They pray longer.

They shrink deeper.

All to keep the affirmation flowing.

But here's the truth:

Affirmation never healed you because it was never designed to.

It only exposed the places where you were already longing to be seen.

The person who praised you didn't create the wound—they simply touched what was already tender. The high you felt was not love; it was relief. And relief is not the same as healing.

This week, the mirror will turn toward you—not to shame you, but to awaken you.

You will learn to separate the feeling of being chosen from the truth of being worthy.

Key Takeaway

The craving for affirmation was never about them. It was about the parts of you that needed validation long before they arrived.

Reflection Questions for Week 2

Write deeply and honestly. After each answer, add:

"The truth I didn't want to admit here is..."

- When someone praises you, what part of you comes alive—and why?
- Think of a time you were drawn to someone because they made you feel "seen." What wound do you think they were touching?
- How has your desire for affirmation shaped the partners, friends, or circles you chose?
- What do you fear would happen if you stopped needing other people's approval?

Core Exercise 1 – Mapping the Mirror

Choose **three triggers or moments** where someone's words or actions hit you deeply.

For each:

- Describe the moment.

- What emotion you felt immediately.
- What hidden wound it revealed (not enough, abandonment, invisibility, unworthiness, being unchosen).
- What healing action you now know you need.

Do not rush this.

Your triggers are your teachers.

Core Exercise 2 – Rewriting the Reflection

Choose **one recurring trigger** that keeps showing up.

Begin writing with this prompt:

"This moment shows me where I need care, love, and acknowledgment. I honor this part of myself and choose to respond with awareness and compassion..."

Then write:

- What this trigger teaches you
- How you will respond differently
- What you will no longer tolerate
- What your healed self would do

Group Discussion Prompts (Optional)

- Share a moment when affirmation from someone clouded your clarity.
- Discuss how triggers reveal wounds rather than create them.
- Explore how the group can practice validation without dependency.

Action Step – This Week

As soon as you feel triggered or unseen:

1. Pause.

2. Ask: "What is this touching in me?"
3. Give yourself what you were seeking from them (attention, truth, reassurance, safety).
4. At week's end, journal:
5. "How did my triggers teach me instead of torment me?"

Weekly Declaration

Speak boldly every day:

"I see the lessons in my triggers. My wounds are not my shame—they are my awakening."

Daily Regimen for Week 2

Day 1 — Sit With the Scripture and the Craving to Be Seen

- Read Galatians 1:10 three times.
- Write about the first time you remember feeling unseen or overlooked.
- Finish: "When people affirm me, what I secretly hope it proves about me is..."

Day 2 — How the High Hooked You

- Re-read the Weekly Summary.
- Write about one person whose praise felt like a "high."
- Name **three red flags** you ignored because you were chasing affirmation.

Day 3 — Reflection Questions, No Hiding

- Answer all reflection questions for Week 2.
- After each answer, include:
- "The truth I did not want to admit here is..."

Day 4 — The Letter of Validation You've Been Waiting For

Write a letter beginning with:

"I honor the love I have given and the depth of my heart. Even when it felt unreturned, it was never wasted…"

Then:

- Name things about yourself you wish others noticed.
- Affirm them boldly.
- Validate yourself without waiting to be chosen.

Day 5 — One Situation Without Chasing Praise

- Do ONE thing today without telling anyone, posting it, or seeking applause.
- Tonight, journal: "This is what it felt like to do something no one clapped for…"

Day 6 — Where Approval Has Ruled You

- Write the list: "Places where other people's approval rules me."
- For each, write:
- One sentence about the fear behind stopping.
- One sentence of truth to replace the fear.

Day 7 — Weekly Review, Prayer, and Declaration

- Underline the most painful sentence of the week.
- Pray for detox from approval addiction.
- Declare: "I am enough in God. I am enough in truth. I no longer beg to be seen—I stand knowing I am already chosen."

WEEK 3 — FACING THE MIRROR

Your Triggers Are Teachers, Not Just Trauma

Anchor Scripture of the Week

Psalm 139:23–24 (NIV)

"Search me, God, and know my heart; test me and know my anxious thoughts.

See if there is any offensive way in me, and lead me in the way everlasting."

Why this scripture:

This week is about **courageous self-examination**. Triggers are the places where God gently reveals the wounds we've hidden, the fears we've buried, and the patterns we've normalized. Psalm 139 invites God into the deepest chambers of the heart—not to condemn us, but to lead us into healing.

Personal Story of the Week —"The Trigger That Told the Truth"

There was a moment years ago that I thought was about *him*, but it was really about *me*.

We were talking—well, *I* was talking, trying to explain how something he said had hurt me. He sighed, rolled his eyes, and said:

"You're doing too much. It's not that deep."

My chest tightened.

My throat burned.

My heart dropped to my knees.

It felt like he had reached inside me and pressed directly on an old bruise.

I didn't know why it hurt so deeply then.

I thought it was because he was dismissive.

I thought it was because he didn't care.

But later that night, in the quiet, the truth came:

That bruise wasn't his—it was mine.

Long before him, I had learned to shrink my feelings.

Long before him, I was taught that my emotions were "too much."

Long before him, I had swallowed things that needed to be spoken.

He didn't create the wound—

he exposed it.

And that exposure felt like betrayal, but it was actually revelation.

I remember sitting on the edge of my bed whispering:

"God, why does this keep happening to me?"

And the Holy Spirit answered in a way I didn't expect:

"Because you keep responding to the mirror instead of the message."

In that moment, I realized that certain people in our lives are not sent to destroy us—they are sent to **show us ourselves**.

To show us what still hurts.

To show us where the lies live.

To show us what needs healing.

To show us where the little girl inside is still waiting to be acknowledged.

That day, the trigger became my teacher.

And this week, it will become *yours*.

Weekly Focus

This week you will learn to view your emotional triggers not as shameful reactions but as **sacred indicators** of unresolved wounds. Instead of internalizing pain, you will begin to interpret it. Instead of avoiding discomfort, you will explore it.

This is the week the mirror becomes your mentor.

Optional Reading (Companion Book)

Unchained: The Awakening of the Empath's Soul — Chapter 2: The Mirror Effect

Key Truth of the Week

The mirror did not break you—it simply revealed where you were already bleeding.

By the End of Week 3, You Will:

• Identify emotional triggers and locate the wound beneath them.

- Shift from reacting impulsively to responding with awareness.
- Recognize which triggers come from past pain instead of present danger.
- Honor your wounds instead of hiding or hating them.

Part Three – The Mirror Effect

How Unhealthy People Expose What You've Buried

Full Summary

The "mirror effect" is one of the most profound and painful experiences an empath can face. When someone reflects your wounds back to you—intentionally or unintentionally—it can feel like an attack. But in reality, it is exposure. And exposure is the beginning of healing.

Narcissists and emotionally unhealthy people often act as mirrors because they see your vulnerabilities, not to heal them, but to use them. Yet what they reveal is not new pain—it is **old pain resurfacing**.

These triggers—those moments that strike you deeply—are messages.

They reveal:

- Where you fear abandonment
- Where you feel unworthy
- Where you feel invisible
- Where you've been silenced
- Where your inner child is still waiting to be acknowledged

The mirror effect is not about blaming yourself for others' behavior.

It is about recognizing:

"This pain existed in me before they touched it."

And that realization is where your awakening begins.

Once you understand what your triggers are really pointing to, you can begin to meet your own needs, validate your own emotions, and care for yourself in the places where others have failed you.

Key Takeaway

Your triggers are not your enemies—they are your compass.

Reflection Questions for Week 3

After each answer, add:

"The truth I didn't want to admit here is..."

1. Think of a moment when someone's words cut deeper than they should have. What wound did it touch?
2. How have your triggers caused you to doubt your worth or instincts?
3. How can your triggers guide you into healing instead of shame?
4. What would change in your life if you saw triggers as information rather than attacks?

Core Exercise 1 – Mapping the Mirror

Write this in paragraph form:

Choose **3 mirror moments**—times when someone's behavior made you feel:

- hurt
- rejected
- ignored
- dismissed
- embarrassed
- afraid

For each moment, write:

- What happened
- What emotion rose first
- What hidden wound it exposed (fear of abandonment, unworthiness, "not enough," invisibility, rejection)
- What healing action you now know you need (truth, boundaries, compassion, reassurance, inner child care)

This is deep work—it will change the way you see yourself.

Core Exercise 2 – Rewriting the Reflection

Choose **one recurring trigger**—the one that follows you into relationships, friendships, or family dynamics.

Write:

"This moment shows me where I need care, love, and acknowledgment. I honor this part of myself. I refuse to hate my wounds. Instead, I will listen to what they are asking me for..."

Then list **practical actions** you will take next time the trigger shows up:

- Will you pause?
- Will you self-soothe?
- Will you speak up?
- Will you set a boundary?
- Will you remind yourself of the truth?

Awareness is the beginning of mastery.

Group Discussion Prompts (Optional)

- Share a moment when you realized your reaction was about an old wound, not the new situation.
- Discuss how triggers can guide healing rather than create chaos.
- Explore ways the group can support each other in responding with compassion rather than judgment.

Action Step – This Week

Every time you feel triggered:

1. Pause before reacting.
2. Ask: "What is this really touching in me?"
3. Give yourself what you were subconsciously hoping to get from them.
4. At week's end, journal:
5. "This is what my triggers taught me this week..."

Weekly Declaration

Speak aloud daily:

"I see the lessons in my triggers. My wounds are not my shame—they are my path to awakening."

Daily Regimen for Week 3

Day 1 — Sit With the Scripture and the Mirror

- Read Psalm 139:23–24 slowly three times.
- Write about the first time you remember feeling "exposed" emotionally.
- Finish:

"The place where I fear being most seen is..."

Day 2 — The Trigger That Told the Truth

- Re-read the Weekly Summary.
- Write about one moment when someone's behavior cut you deeply.
- List **three ways** that moment revealed an old wound.

Day 3 — Reflection Questions, No Hiding

- Answer all reflection questions.
- After each, write:

"The truth I didn't want to admit here is..."

Day 4 — A Letter to the Wounded Part of You

Write:

"I see you. I know why you react the way you do. I'm not angry with you for being triggered—I'm here to understand you..."

Affirm your inner self.

Acknowledge the wound, not the shame.

Day 5 — Pause Instead of Reacting

Today, commit to pausing at least once when triggered.

Tonight, journal:

"This is what I discovered when I paused instead of reacting..."

Day 6 — What My Triggers Have Cost Me

Write:

"Because I didn't understand my triggers, I paid the price in these ways..."

Then write:

"I refuse to let unhealed wounds run my life anymore."

Day 7 — Weekly Review, Prayer, and Declaration

- Review the week's writings.
- Pray:
- "Lord, help me see my wounds with compassion, not shame."
- Declare:
- "My triggers are my teachers. I awaken with every revelation."

WEEK 4 — HEALING THE STARVED HEART

No More Loving Until You Disappear

Anchor Scripture of the Week

Proverbs 4:23 (NIV)

"Above all else, guard your heart, for everything you do flows from it."

Why this scripture:

A starved heart is an unguarded heart—a heart that has poured and poured until nothing remained. As you learn to stop giving from emptiness and begin nourishing yourself, this scripture becomes your shield, your reminder, and your permission:

Your heart is worthy of protection, preservation, and priority.

Personal Story of the Week —"The Day I Realized I Was Disappearing"

There was a season in my life when I mistook self-erasure for love.

If he needed money, I gave it.

If he needed comfort, I carried it.

If he needed reassurance, I poured it.

If he needed space, I shrank myself small enough to disappear.

I thought I was being loving.

I thought I was being loyal.

I thought I was doing what a "good woman" does.

But the truth was this:

Every time I showed up for him, I was abandoning myself.

It crept up slowly at first—little compromises that didn't look harmful:

"I'll cancel my plans."

"I'll figure it out."

"It's okay, I don't need anything."

"You go ahead, I'll manage."

But the more I gave, the more he expected.

And the more he expected, the less I recognized myself.

One day, I looked in the mirror and didn't see a woman—

I saw a **shell**.

Empty eyes.

A quiet voice.

A tired soul that had fed everyone but herself.

That day, the Holy Spirit whispered something that shook me:

"You don't love him. You love the version of yourself you're hoping to earn back through him."

I froze.

Because deep down, I knew it was true.

My giving wasn't compassion—it was desperation.

My sacrifice wasn't love—it was fear.

My devotion wasn't holy—it was bondage masquerading as righteousness.

I had been starving my own heart to feed someone who was never going to pour back into me.

That moment broke me...

But it also awakened me.

I realized:

True love does not require you to disappear to keep it.

True love does not drain you.

True love does not demand your silence, your exhaustion, or your identity.

And now, this week, you are stepping into that same revelation.

Weekly Focus

This week you will confront the ways your heart has been starving—not for the love of others, but for your own love, attention, protection, and compassion. You will uncover the places where you have given from depletion rather than overflow and begin learning what it means to nourish yourself spiritually and emotionally.

This is the week you reclaim the parts of yourself you abandoned to keep someone else comfortable.

Optional Reading (Companion Book)

Unchained: The Awakening of the Empath's Soul — Chapter 3: Starved Hearts

Key Truth of the Week

Giving without receiving is not love—it is bondage.

By the End of Week 4, You Will:

- Identify where your giving has come from emptiness, not abundance.
- Recognize the emotional and spiritual cost of self-abandonment.
- Begin to nourish your heart instead of starving it.
- Understand the difference between holy sacrifice and unhealthy self-erasure.

Part Four – Starved Hearts

Why You Kept Giving Even When You Felt Empty

Full Summary

Empaths often carry an instinctive, God-given ability to love deeply, give generously, and nurture compassionately. But when this gift is misdirected, manipulated, or unreciprocated, it becomes a trap—a cycle of pouring into others while quietly bleeding out inside.

At first, the giving feels noble, even sacred.

You show up.

You forgive.

You extend grace.

You offer comfort.

You become the safe place everyone runs to.

But slowly, something shifts.

Your giving stops being an act of love and becomes a survival mechanism.

You give because you're afraid to lose them.

You give because you fear being replaced.

You give because validating them feels easier than valuing yourself.

You give because their need for you distracts you from your own emptiness.

This is the starved heart.

A heart that keeps feeding others while silently begging to be fed.

A heart that keeps showing up for everyone except itself.

A heart that confuses depletion with devotion.

But here is the turning point:

Your heart isn't starving for another person's love—it's starving for your own.

Healing begins when you acknowledge that giving from emptiness is not holy, noble, or loving. It is bondage.

True love—God's love—flows from fullness, not exhaustion.

This is the week you learn to reconnect to that wellspring.

Key Takeaway

Your heart was never meant to live on leftovers.

Reflection Questions for Week 4

After each answer, write:

"The truth I didn't want to admit here is..."

1. Recall a time when your giving felt endless. What were you afraid would happen if you stopped?
2. How has someone's manipulation or emotional need reshaped your identity?
3. What patterns in your giving reveal where your heart was starving?
4. What does self-love, protection, and nourishment look like for you right now?

Core Exercise 1 – Identifying the Cage

Write this in narrative form:

Choose **3 relationships or situations** where you gave more than you had emotionally, financially, physically, or spiritually.

For each:

- Describe how you gave
- Explain how it drained you
- Identify what that experience taught you about true love, boundaries, and self-worth

Be unfiltered.

This is how the cage opens.

Core Exercise 2 – Letter to Your Heart

Begin with:

"Dear Heart, I honor the love you gave and the pain you endured. You have carried more than you should have, stayed longer than you deserved, and starved while feeding others. From this day forward, I refuse to starve you..."

Then list **three specific ways** you will nourish your heart this week:

- Rest
- Joy
- Therapy
- Saying no
- Pulling back
- Setting boundaries
- Prioritizing yourself

End with a promise:

"I will not abandon you again."

Group Discussion Prompts (Optional)

- Share a moment when you realized your giving had become a cage.
- Discuss how a starved heart chooses people who take rather than give.
- Explore how nourishing yourself changes the way you give to others.

Action Step – This Week

Identify **one relationship or role** where you consistently over-give.
This week:

- Pull back one notch
- Observe what happens
- Notice how you feel when you honor your limits

At week's end, journal:
"What did I discover when I stopped over-functioning?"

Weekly Declaration

Speak aloud daily:
"My heart is no longer starving. I receive the love I once begged for. I am full, I am worthy, I am free."

Daily Regimen for Week 4

Day 1 — Sit With the Scripture and Your Starved Heart

- Read Proverbs 4:23 three times.
- Write about a moment when you realized you were giving more than you had.
- Finish:

"The place where I feel the most depleted is…"

Day 2 — When Giving Became a Cage

- Re-read the Weekly Summary.
- Write about one relationship where giving was endless.
- Name three ways it drained your identity, your energy, or your spirit.

Day 3 — Reflection Questions, No Hiding

- Answer the reflection questions for Week 4.
- After each, write:

"The truth I didn't want to admit here is..."

Day 4 — The Letter Your Heart Has Been Waiting For

Write the full **Letter to Your Heart**.
Do not rush.
Let your heart speak—this is how healing begins.

Day 5 — Pull Back One Notch

Choose one situation where you over-give.
Pull back today.
Tonight, journal:
"This is what I felt when I didn't show up the way I usually do..."

Day 6 — What Starvation Has Cost You

Write:
"Because I ignored my heart, I paid the price in these ways..."
Then acknowledge:
"I refuse to keep starving myself for love."

Day 7 — Weekly Review, Prayer, and Declaration

- Review what you wrote this week.
- Pray:

"God, teach me to feed my heart the love I once demanded from others."

- Declare boldly:

"My heart is full. My boundaries are holy. My love is no longer for sale."

WEEK 5 — BREAKING THE ADDICTION TO GIVING

Survival Masquerading as Love

Anchor Scripture of the Week

Galatians 5:1 (NIV)

"It is for freedom that Christ has set us free. Stand firm, then, and do not let yourselves be burdened again by a yoke of slavery."

Why this scripture:

This week confronts a hard truth: when giving becomes compulsive, it is no longer love—it is bondage. Galatians 5:1 reminds us that freedom is not optional in Christ. Any relationship that requires self-erasure, silence, or emotional slavery is not aligned with God's design for love.

Personal Story of the Week —"The Day I Realized Love Had Become Survival"

There was a moment when I finally admitted the truth—

I wasn't giving because I wanted to.

I was giving because I was afraid.

Afraid that if I stopped explaining, he would leave.

Afraid that if I said no, I would be rejected.

Afraid that if I stopped shrinking, I would be alone.

I remember thinking, *If I can just hold on a little longer, maybe it will turn into love.*

But it didn't.

The more I gave, the more he demanded.

The quieter I became, the louder his needs grew.

The more I sacrificed, the emptier I felt.

One night, exhausted and numb, I whispered to God:

"Why does this feel like I'm disappearing?"

And the answer came gently but firmly:

"Because this is no longer love. This is survival."

That truth hurt—but it freed me.

Because love does not require you to vanish in order to stay connected.

Weekly Focus

This week is about recognizing when love has shifted into survival mode. You will begin to identify where giving stopped being a choice and became a compulsion—where fear, not love, started driving your behavior.

This is the week you stop feeding relationships that consume your soul.

Optional Reading (Companion Book)

Unchained: The Awakening of the Empath's Soul — Chapter 5: The Transaction Masquerading as Love

Key Truth of the Week

Love given from emptiness is not love—it is self-destruction.

By the End of Week 5, You Will:

- Recognize when giving became compulsion, not choice
- Identify how your voice and identity were silenced
- Begin reclaiming your voice and sense of self
- Understand the difference between love and survival
- Break the illusion of transactional bonding

Part Five — The Transaction

When Fear Replaces Love

Full Summary

What an empath often experiences as love in a narcissistic relationship is frequently survival disguised as devotion. Fear fuels the giving—fear of abandonment, fear of being unseen, fear of not being enough.

The narcissist initially mirrors affection, attention, and intimacy, creating the illusion of love. Over time, affection becomes conditional and the empath finds herself bargaining for crumbs of connection.

This transactional dynamic drains joy, silences voice, and slowly erodes identity. When the illusion finally shatters, the devastation reveals a holy exposure: love rooted in fear is bondage, not covenant.

Awakening begins when the empath recognizes the counterfeit and steps toward love that is mutual, safe, and life-giving.

Key Takeaway

Survival disguised as love is bondage. Awakening begins when you recognize the transaction and reclaim your worth.

Reflection Questions for Week 5

After each answer, add:
"The truth I didn't want to admit here is..."

1. Reflect on a relationship where you stayed out of fear rather than love. What fear kept you bound?
2. How did bargaining, excusing, or silencing yourself affect your emotional and spiritual health?
3. What signs revealed that love had become transactional?
4. How does recognizing the difference between survival and love help you reclaim your heart?

Core Exercise 1 — Mapping the Bond

Choose one significant relationship or situation. Write in paragraph form:

- How you gave (bending, shrinking, complying)
- Where you felt drained or controlled
- What you learned about yourself through the pattern

This exercise reveals where your generosity was being exploited rather than honored.

Core Exercise 2 — Reclaiming Voice and Identity

Write:

"I see the ways I gave too much and the ways my spirit was silenced.
I reclaim my voice, my identity, and my power..."
Then list **three actions** you will take this week to honor your voice (e.g., stating a preference, saying no, speaking truth gently but firmly).

Action Step — This Week

Notice every time you want to say *"It's fine"* when it's not.
Instead, practice one honest statement:
"This doesn't work for me."
At week's end, journal:
"How did it feel to hear my own voice again?"

Weekly Declaration

Speak aloud daily:
"My voice is rising. My identity is returning.
I am not a supply source for broken people.
I give from fullness, not bondage.
I am a whole woman with a sound mind and a powerful voice."

Daily Regimen for Week 5

Day 1 — Scripture & Compulsive Giving

- Read Galatians 5:1
- Write about a recent time you said yes but wanted to say no
- Finish:

"The real reason I said yes was because I was afraid that..."

Day 2 — Seeing Your Own Addiction

- Re-read the Weekly Summary
- Journal how giving slowly became survival
- Write one sentence that starts with:

"I hate admitting this, but..."

Day 3 — Reflection Questions in the Mirror

- Answer all reflection questions
- After each, write:

"I was giving from fullness, fear, or emptiness."

Day 4 — Letter to Your Silenced Voice

Write:

"I see the ways I gave too much and the ways my spirit was silenced..."
Name the moments you swallowed words.
Write what you wish you had said.

Day 5 — One Brave 'No'

- Identify one place you usually over-give
- Practice a simple "no" or "not this time"
- At night, journal how it felt in your body and emotions

Day 6 — Who I Am Without Over-Giving

Finish this sentence **10 times**:

"I am still valuable even if I don't..."
Let your worth detach from performance.

Day 7 — Weekly Review, Prayer, and Declaration

- Review the week's insights
- Pray:

"Lord, help me honor my limits without guilt."

- Declare:

"My giving is a gift, not a leash. I give from love, not fear."

WEEK 6 — WHEN EMPATHY BECOMES A CAGE

Exposing Counterfeit Love: Survival Is Not Love

Anchor Scripture of the Week

Matthew 11:28–30 (NIV)

"Come to me, all you who are weary and burdened, and I will give you rest...

For my yoke is easy and my burden is light."

Why this scripture:

This week confronts the lie that love is supposed to exhaust you. Jesus makes it clear: anything that crushes your spirit, erases your voice, or leaves you depleted is not from Him. If your empathy has become heavy, enslaving, or suffocating, it is no longer operating in truth—it has been hijacked.

Personal Story of the Week —"When My Empathy Became My Prison"

There was a season when I believed my empathy was proof of my maturity.

If I could just understand him more...

If I could just be patient longer...

If I could just see his wounds instead of my own pain...

Then maybe I was being Christlike.

But something was wrong.

I was exhausted—spiritually, emotionally, physically.

I kept telling myself I was loving, but inside I felt trapped.

My compassion had turned into obligation.

My understanding had turned into silence.

My empathy had turned into a cage.

I remember thinking, *If I leave, I'm abandoning him.*

But the Holy Spirit interrupted that lie and said:

"You are not abandoning him—you are rescuing yourself."

That was the moment I realized something sobering:

Empathy without boundaries doesn't save anyone.

It only sacrifices you.

And God never asked me to destroy myself to prove my love.

Weekly Focus

This week exposes how empathy—when misused—can become bondage instead of blessing. You will begin to identify where compassion turned into self-erasure and where understanding replaced accountability.

This is the week you stop calling endurance "love" and start calling it what it is: survival.

Optional Reading (Companion Book)

Unchained: The Awakening of the Empath's Soul — Chapter 6: When Empathy Becomes a Cage

Key Truth of the Week

If you must constantly bargain to be loved, you are not loved—you are being managed.

By the End of Week 6, You Will:

- Identify relationships where empathy was used against you
- Recognize how survival shaped your decisions
- Understand the difference between compassion and self-erasure
- Begin choosing love that frees, not love that cages
- Restore empathy as a strength—not a liability

Part Six — The Cage

How a Sacred Gift Became Bondage

Full Summary

Empathy is a sacred gift—the ability to feel deeply, connect authentically, and love with sincerity. But in the hands of emotionally unhealthy people, empathy becomes leverage. The narcissist exploits compassion, turning it into obligation, guilt, and silence.

The empath begins to excuse harm, justify disrespect, and diminish herself—all in the name of understanding. But this is not Christlike love. This is bondage.

Awakening begins when the empath realizes empathy was never meant to imprison. God calls His daughters to redirect compassion inward, to honor their limits, protect their voice, and restore their strength. True empathy uplifts both people. It does not require self-destruction.

Key Takeaway

Empathy misused can imprison—but redirected, it restores, strengthens, and empowers.

Reflection Questions for Week 6

After each answer, add:
"This is where I have been confusing love with survival…"

1. Reflect on a time when your empathy was exploited. How did it impact your sense of self?
2. How did you justify behavior that diminished your own needs?
3. What patterns reveal when empathy becomes bondage instead of a gift?
4. How does redirecting empathy inward strengthen your voice, identity, and spirit?

Core Exercise 1 — Mapping the Cage

Choose one relationship or situation. Write in paragraph form:

- How your empathy was used against you
- How it made you feel (drained, guilty, trapped, anxious)
- Where you ignored your own needs
- What reclaiming power would look like now

Core Exercise 2 — Restoring Your Empathy

Write:

"I honor the depth of my empathy and the ways it has been exploited.

Today, I reclaim my gift and redirect it toward my own healing and purpose..."

Then list **three actions** you will take this week to nurture yourself with the same care you once gave others.

Action Step — This Week

Identify one area where your empathy has been giving without return.

Redirect that compassion inward through:

- a boundary
- rest
- honesty
- self-care
- prayer

Journal:

"How did honoring myself change the way I felt in my body and spirit?"

Weekly Declaration

Speak aloud daily:

"My empathy is my power, not my prison.
I give from fullness, not obligation.
I honor my needs without guilt.
I am free to love without losing myself."

Daily Regimen for Week 6

Day 1 — Scripture & Survival Mode

- Read Matthew 11:28–30
- Write about a time you stayed because you feared being alone
- Finish:

"I told myself I was staying because of love, but the truth is..."

Day 2 — Seeing the Transaction

- Re-read the Weekly Summary
- Journal one transaction-based relationship
- Identify where fear drove you more than love

Day 3 — Reflection Questions, Hard and Holy

- Answer all reflection questions
- Then write:

"This is how survival has shaped my decisions..."

Day 4 — Letter of Holy Exposure

Write:

"I see the ways I gave to survive and the pain it caused..."

Name the illusions you are releasing:

- that you're unlovable
- that this is normal
- that love requires suffering

Day 5 — One Choice Out of Love, Not Fear

- Make one decision today from peace, not panic
- Journal how it felt in your body and soul

Day 6 — Writing Your Non-Negotiables

Write two lists:

- What Love Will No Longer Cost Me:

(my sanity, sleep, safety, purpose, walk with God)

- What Real Love Will Include:

(respect, honesty, accountability, consistency)

Day 7 — Weekly Review, Prayer, and Declaration

- Review the lies you exposed
- Pray:

"Lord, help me love without self-betrayal."

- Declare:

"I release the counterfeit. I refuse to bargain for love. I am worthy of holy love that does not require my destruction."

WEEK 7 — THE HOLY DISRUPTION

When God Allows the Breaking for Your Awakening

Anchor Scripture of the Week

Romans 8:28 (NIV)

"And we know that in all things God works for the good of those who love Him, who have been called according to His purpose."

Why This Scripture

This week reframes devastation. What looked like loss, betrayal, and abandonment was not the absence of God—it was His intervention. Romans 8:28 anchors us in this truth: God does not waste pain. Even the breaking becomes material for awakening.

Personal Story of the Week —"When the Breaking Didn't Destroy Me"

There was a moment when everything collapsed at once.

The lies surfaced.

The masks fell.

The relationship I had fought so hard to save shattered.

I remember crying out, not just in pain—but in confusion:

"God, why didn't You stop this?"

I had prayed. I had hoped. I had believed that love, patience, and faith would change him. But instead of rescue, I got ruin.

For a while, I believed God had abandoned me.

But later—after the dust settled and the silence stretched—I realized something I could not see while I was inside the storm:

The bond itself was the prison.

God didn't break the relationship to hurt me.

He broke it to free me.

What felt like devastation was mercy in disguise.

What felt like loss was the beginning of awakening.

Weekly Focus

This week is about understanding **holy disruption**—the moment when God allows what you were clinging to fall apart because it was holding you captive.

You will begin to see that the breaking was not abandonment, punishment, or failure. It was divine intervention.

This is the week devastation is reinterpreted as deliverance.

Optional Reading (Companion Book)

Unchained: The Awakening of the Empath's Soul — Chapter 7

The Holy Disruption

Key Truth of the Week

The disruption you experienced was God's mercy, not His absence.

By the End of Week 7, You Will:

- Identify disruptions God allowed to free you
- Reframe pain as preparation, not punishment
- Release attachment to what could not go forward with you
- Begin trusting God's strategy even when it hurts

- See the breaking as the birthplace of awakening

Part Seven — The Disruption

When God Breaks What Cannot Be Healed

Full Summary

When the empath's bond with a narcissist collapses, it often feels like betrayal—not only by the person, but by God Himself. The prayers went unanswered. The rescue never came. The relationship ended in devastation.

But this breaking was not abandonment.

God allowed the disruption because the bond itself was the prison.

What felt destructive was actually strategic.

What felt like silence was precision.

What felt like loss was mercy in disguise.

The holy disruption strips away what no longer serves you and reveals the true self beneath survival. Through the breaking, God awakens an empath who no longer gives from emptiness, a daughter who receives validation from Him alone, and a soul prepared to walk in freedom.

This disruption is not the end—it is an invitation. Pain becomes seed. Breaking becomes birthing. And devastation becomes awakening.

Key Takeaway

God did not break you—He broke what was breaking you.

Reflection Questions for Week 7

After each answer, write:

"What God was protecting me from was..."

1. Reflect on a disruption in your life that felt devastating at the time. What

do you see differently now?
2. How did God's silence during the breaking actually create clarity and awakening?
3. In what ways were you clinging to something that was holding you in bondage?
4. How does viewing disruption as mercy change how you grieve loss?

Core Exercise 1 — Seeing the Holy Disruption

Choose one major breaking or loss. Write in paragraph form:

- What was disrupted or lost
- How you initially felt
- What you now see God protecting you from
- What the disruption awakened in you
- How this breaking changed your direction

Core Exercise 2 — Birth in the Breaking

Write a letter to yourself **from God's perspective**.
Begin with:
"Daughter, I allowed this disruption not to harm you, but to awaken you…"
Let the letter affirm your worth, identity, and freedom.
Then answer:

- Three ways you will embrace this awakening spiritually
- Three ways emotionally
- Three ways relationally

End with:
"This is how the breaking gave birth to my becoming."

Action Step — This Week

Identify one area where you are resisting necessary change.

- Release control through prayer or surrender
- Take one small step toward trust instead of fear
- Journal at week's end:

"What shifted when I stopped fighting the disruption?"

Weekly Declaration

Speak aloud daily:
"I trust the holy disruption.
I release what could not go with me.
God is not punishing me—He is freeing me.
Even in the breaking, I am held, restored, and becoming whole."

Daily Regimen for Week 7

Day 1 — Scripture & the Breaking

- Read Romans 8:28 slowly
- Write about a breaking that confused or devastated you
- Finish:

"At the time, I thought this ruined me, but now I see…"

Day 2 — Naming the Disruption

- Re-read the Weekly Summary
- Journal about what truly ended—was it love, or was it survival?
- Write:

"What God dismantled was…"

Day 3 — Reflection Questions, No Resistance

- Answer all reflection questions
- After each, write:

"This disruption was preparing me for…"

Day 4 — Letter From God

- Write the full letter from Core Exercise 2
- Sit quietly after writing and receive what was revealed

Day 5 — Surrender Instead of Control

- Identify where you are still trying to "fix" what God already broke
- Write:

"What happens when I stop trying to resurrect what God buried?"

Day 6 — What the Breaking Birthed

Write a paragraph titled:
"Because This Fell Apart, I Awakened To…"

Day 7 — Weekly Review, Prayer, and Declaration

- Review your writings
- Pray:

"God, help me trust You when I don't understand."

- Declare:

"The breaking was the making. I am awakening."

WEEK 8 — THE SILENCE OF GOD

Finding Presence, Purpose, and Strength in God's Quiet

Anchor Scripture of the Week

1 Kings 19:11–12 (NIV)

"The Lord said, 'Go out and stand on the mountain in the presence of the Lord, for the Lord is about to pass by.'

Then a great and powerful wind tore the mountains apart… but the Lord was not in the wind.

After the wind there was an earthquake, but the Lord was not in the earthquake.

After the earthquake came a fire, but the Lord was not in the fire.

And after the fire came a gentle whisper."

Why This Scripture

This week teaches you how God speaks when everything else goes quiet. The empath is accustomed to noise—emotional intensity, constant reassurance, reaction, pursuit. But God often removes the noise so His voice can finally be heard. Silence is not abandonment; it is intimacy.

Personal Story of the Week —"When God Said Nothing… and Changed Everything"

After the disruption, I expected God to explain Himself.

I thought there would be clarity immediately.

Answers.

Relief.

A sense of *"See? I told you so."*

Instead, there was silence.

No instructions.

No reassurance.

No emotional rush to replace what was gone.

At first, the silence terrified me.

I wondered if I had failed Him.

If I had misunderstood everything.

If the quiet meant I was alone now.

But slowly—painfully—I realized something sacred:

God wasn't gone.

He was closer than He had ever been.

The silence was stripping away the voices that once defined me.

The chaos that kept me distracted.

The emotional noise that kept me dependent.

In the quiet, I learned how to breathe again.

How to listen without panic.

How to exist without needing to be chosen.

The silence didn't break me.

It rebuilt me.

Weekly Focus

This week reframes silence.

You will learn that God's quiet seasons are not rejection, delay, or neglect. They are sacred spaces where identity is restored, dependence is recalibrated, and strength is formed.

This is the week the wilderness becomes holy ground.

Optional Reading (Companion Book)

Unchained: The Awakening of the Empath's Soul — Chapter 8

The Silence of God

Key Truth of the Week

God's silence is not rejection—it is sacred space for awakening, growth, and strength.

By the End of Week 8, You Will:

- Stop interpreting silence as abandonment
- Learn to hear God with your spirit instead of your anxiety
- Develop trust without constant reassurance
- Strengthen identity apart from validation
- Recognize quiet as preparation, not punishment

Part Eight — The Silence

Where God Rebuilds What Was Broken

Full Summary

After heartbreak and disruption, God's silence can feel unbearable—especially for the empath, who is wired for connection, affirmation, and emotional responsiveness. The absence of noise is often mistaken for absence of love.

But silence is not emptiness.

It is sacred space.

In the quiet, God strips away distractions and false dependencies. Every unseen tear, every unanswered prayer, every lonely moment is held and transformed by Him. Silence becomes strength as trust deepens, identity stabilizes, and resilience is formed.

What feels like loss is actually preparation.
What feels like isolation is transformation.
What feels like nothing is becoming everything.

Key Takeaway

The quiet is not where you are forgotten—it is where you are rebuilt.

Reflection Questions for Week 8

After each answer, write:

"What this silence is teaching me is..."

1. How have you experienced God's silence in your life, and what emotions did it stir?
2. In what ways did you confuse silence with abandonment or rejection?
3. How has stillness helped you develop strength, clarity, or discernment?
4. What is God forming in you during this quiet season?

Core Exercise 1 — Listening in the Silence

Choose one season of silence. Write in paragraph form:

- What was silent (relationship, prayer life, clarity, answers)
- What emotions surfaced
- What you now sense God teaching you
- How you can respond in faith instead of fear

Core Exercise 2 — Journaling Through the Wilderness

Write a letter to God.
Begin with:
"Lord, I feel unseen, unheard, and abandoned. Yet I choose to trust You..."
Write honestly. Do not censor grief or doubt.
Then answer:

- Three ways you will honor stillness this week
- Three ways you will quiet anxiety instead of chasing reassurance
- Three ways silence can become sacred rather than threatening

Action Step — This Week

Identify one area where you are pushing for answers instead of trusting God.

- Practice stillness instead of striving
- Sit with discomfort without fixing it
- Journal at week's end:

"What changed when I stopped demanding noise?"

Weekly Declaration

Speak aloud daily:
"I trust the silence.
God is near, not absent.
In the stillness, I am being strengthened, not forgotten.
My soul is awakening in the quiet."

Daily Regimen for Week 8

Day 1 — Scripture & the Quiet

- Read 1 Kings 19:11–12 slowly
- Write about a silence that frightened you
- Finish:

"I assumed God was absent because..."

Day 2 — Mercy in the Quiet

- Re-read the Weekly Summary
- Journal what noise God may have been protecting you from
- Write:

"The silence saved me from..."

Day 3 — Reflection Questions, Stillness Style

- Answer all reflection questions
- Then write:

"If I trusted God more here, I would..."

Day 4 — Letter From the Wilderness

- Write a letter to God expressing doubt and trust
- Sit quietly after writing—no music, no phone, no distraction

Day 5 — One Act of Stillness

- Choose one moment today to do nothing
- No fixing, no explaining, no proving
- Journal how your body and spirit responded

Day 6 — Identity Without Noise

Write a paragraph titled:
"Who I Am When No One Is Affirming Me"

Day 7 — Weekly Review, Prayer, and Declaration

- Review your writings
- Pray:

"God, teach me to trust You in the quiet."

- Declare:

"I am not abandoned. I am being prepared."

WEEK 9 — THE EXPOSURE

The Breaking Was the Making

Anchor Scripture of the Week

John 8:32 (NIV)

"Then you will know the truth, and the truth will set you free."

Why This Scripture

Exposure is painful, but it is never pointless. Truth does not arrive to shame you—it comes to free you. This week centers on the moment when illusion collapses and clarity rises. God allows exposure not to humiliate you, but to liberate you from what could no longer remain hidden.

Personal Story of the Week —"When the Illusion Finally Fell"

The exposure didn't come gently.

There was no soft revelation or quiet understanding.

It came like a storm—sudden, undeniable, irreversible.

One moment I was still trying to make sense of things, still explaining away behaviors, still believing there was something I could fix. And then—everything unraveled. The words didn't match the actions anymore. The excuses collapsed. The truth stood exposed, bare and undeniable.

What hurt most wasn't just seeing *him* clearly.

It was seeing *myself*.

I saw how much I had tolerated.

How much I had silenced.

How much of myself I had reshaped just to survive.

At first, the exposure felt like humiliation.

Like failure.

Like I had been foolish for so long.

But in the quiet aftermath, God whispered something that changed everything:

"This isn't your ending. This is your awakening."

What I thought was destruction was actually deliverance.

What I thought was loss was really release.

The exposure wasn't there to break me—it was there to break the chains.

Weekly Focus

This week is about **truth without denial**.

You will confront what was hidden, distorted, or minimized—not to dwell in pain, but to reclaim your power. Exposure ends confusion, dissolves soul ties, and dismantles false identities that were formed in survival.

This is the week illusion dies—and freedom begins.

Optional Reading (Companion Book)

Unchained: The Awakening of the Empath's Soul — Chapter 9

The Exposure: The Breaking Was the Making

Key Truth of the Week

Exposure is not destruction—it is deliverance.

By the End of Week 9, You Will:

- Identify moments where truth replaced illusion
- Recognize false identities formed in survival
- Begin releasing unhealthy soul ties
- Anchor your worth in God instead of validation
- Honor the lesson without returning to the bondage

Part Nine — The Exposure

When Truth Ends the Bond

Full Summary

Exposure is the moment the veil is lifted.

What once felt like love is revealed as bondage. What once felt confusing becomes clear. God allows the empath to see—not only the narcissist's true nature, but her own hidden strength.

The paradigm shift happens when validation is no longer sought from people, but received from God. False identities are dismantled. Survival roles are released. Soul ties weaken and begin to break.

The exposure is not your failure—it is your freedom.

It is not the end of your story—it is the sacred beginning of awakening, empowerment, and wholeness.

Key Takeaway

The breaking exposed the truth—but it also revealed who you are becoming.

Reflection Questions for Week 9

After each answer, write:
"What I can see clearly now is..."

1. How have you experienced exposure in relationships—seeing truths you were once blind to?
2. What false identities or roles did you adopt to survive (peacemaker, fixer, savior, silent one)?
3. In what ways has God used the breaking to reveal your strength and worth?
4. How can you honor the lesson without reopening the door to the bondage?

Core Exercise 1 — Identifying the False Self & Soul Ties

Complete the chart below honestly:

False Identity / Belief
How It Served the Bond
What God Is Replacing It With
Steps to Release

Objective:
Recognize the version of yourself created for survival—and begin replacing it with truth rooted in God.

Core Exercise 2 — Love Letter From God Reflection

Slowly read the Love Letter from God included in your book.
Then journal:

- Which words or phrases resonated most deeply?
- Which promises felt hardest to receive—and why?
- Where do you still struggle to believe you are free?

Now write your personal response to God:

"Father, I see the chains You've broken. I acknowledge the freedom You are revealing in me..."

Action Step — This Week

- Identify one soul tie, belief, or pattern that is ready to be released
- Use prayer, journaling, or visualization to symbolically break it
- Track emotional shifts—clarity, relief, grief, strength—without judgment

Journal at week's end:

"This is how freedom feels different than survival..."

Weekly Declaration

Speak aloud daily:

"I am unchained.
The exposure was not my end—it was my awakening.
God has revealed my worth, my strength, and my freedom.
I release what was never mine to carry.
I walk free."

Daily Regimen for Week 9

Day 1 — Scripture & Exposure

- Read John 8:32 slowly
- Write about a moment truth shattered an illusion
- Finish:

"When the truth came out, I felt..."

Day 2 — Redefining the Breaking

- Re-read the Weekly Summary
- Journal how exposure protected you from further harm
- Write:

"If I had not seen the truth, I would have lost..."

Day 3 — Reflection Questions, Fully Awake

- Answer all reflection questions
- Write a paragraph titled:

"What I Refuse to Unsee"

Day 4 — Letter of Release

- Write a letter releasing the false self you no longer need
- Thank her for surviving
- Tell her she can rest now

Day 5 — One Truth-Based Choice

- Make one decision today based on clarity, not fear
- Journal how choosing truth felt in your body and spirit

Day 6 — Evidence of Growth

- Write:

"Here is how I know I am no longer who I was..."

Day 7 — Weekly Review, Prayer, and Declaration

- Review your writing
- Pray:

"God, help me honor the truth without returning to the cage."

- Declare:

"What was exposed no longer has power over me."

WEEK 10 — SACRIFICIAL VS. SELF-DESTRUCTIVE LOVE

Declaring Liberty Over the Empath's Soul

Anchor Scripture of the Week

John 10:10 (NIV)

"The thief comes only to steal and kill and destroy; I have come that they may have life, and have it to the full."

Why This Scripture

This verse draws a clear line between what destroys and what gives life. Love that drains, silences, and diminishes you does not come from God. His love restores, protects, and multiplies life. This week is about learning the difference—and choosing liberty.

Personal Story of the Week —"When Sacrifice Crossed the Line"

For a long time, I told myself I was just being loving.

I called it sacrifice.

I called it loyalty.

I called it being Christlike.

But if I'm honest, what I was really doing was disappearing.

I gave past my limits.

I stayed past my warnings.
I endured things God never asked me to endure.
And every time my soul whispered, *This hurts,* I answered back with guilt:
"Love is supposed to hurt."
"Jesus sacrificed."
"God will honor this."
But one day, clarity broke through the fog.
God didn't ask me to destroy myself.
He asked me to love from fullness—not emptiness.
To give from abundance—not obligation.
That was the day I realized:
I wasn't being sacrificial. I was being self-destructive.
And love—real love—never requires your extinction.

Weekly Focus

This week is about **discernment and declaration**.

You will examine where love crossed into self-betrayal, where sacrifice became survival, and where boundaries were mistaken for selfishness. You will begin reclaiming liberty over your heart, your energy, and your identity.

This is the week you learn how to love **without losing yourself**.

Optional Reading (Companion Book)

Unchained: The Awakening of the Empath's Soul — Chapter 10
Sacrificial vs. Self-Destructive Love

Key Truth of the Week

Love that demands your destruction is not love—it is bondage.

By the End of Week 10, You Will:

- Distinguish sacrificial love from self-destructive giving
- Identify patterns where boundaries were absent
- Begin declaring liberty over your soul
- Replace guilt-driven giving with God-centered love
- Walk more confidently in freedom and wholeness

Part Ten — Declaring Liberty

When Love Stops Costing You Your Soul

Full Summary

True love sets free. It heals. It builds up.

Self-destructive love, however, depletes, silences, and cages the heart. Many empaths confuse suffering with sacrifice, believing that endurance equals holiness. But God's design for love was never meant to crush you.

Sacrificial love flows from abundance and alignment with God. Self-destructive love flows from fear, obligation, and the need to be chosen.

This chapter marks the awakening where the empath learns to give **without disappearing**, to set boundaries **without guilt**, and to love as one who is free—not bound.

Key Takeaway

Sacrifice that destroys you is not holy. God's love restores your soul and honors your boundaries.

Reflection Questions for Week 10

After each answer, write:
"This is where liberty is needed."

1. Where in past relationships did you confuse self-destruction with sacrificial love?
2. How has God been teaching you to recognize the difference between holy giving and harmful giving?
3. What boundaries do you need to establish to protect your heart while still loving fully?
4. Which declarations of liberty resonate most deeply with your soul—and why?

Core Exercise 1 — Identifying Self-Destructive Patterns

Complete the table honestly:

Past Relationship / Situation
Self-Destructive Behavior
Holy Alternative
Next Step

Objective:
Identify where love became self-neglect and replace it with God-honoring, life-giving love.

Core Exercise 2 — Declaring Liberty

Write a personal declaration of freedom over your soul.
You may begin with statements such as:

- "I will no longer confuse sacrifice with self-neglect."
- "I will love, but I will not be consumed."
- "I honor my soul and protect my boundaries without guilt."

Then answer:

- How does it feel to speak these truths aloud?
- What emotions arise as you claim your God-given liberty?

Action Step — This Week

- Identify one relationship or area where your giving has been self-destructive
- Practice establishing one clear, healthy boundary
- Journal the impact on your peace, energy, and confidence

End the week by writing:
"This is how freedom feels in my body and spirit..."

Weekly Declaration

Speak aloud daily:
"I am free.
I am loved.
I am chosen.
I am whole.
I will no longer be chained to counterfeit love.
I love as one who is free—holy, abundant, and empowered."

Daily Regimen for Week 10

Day 1 — Scripture & Discernment

- Read John 10:10 slowly
- Write about a time love drained rather than restored you
- Finish:

"I thought this was love because..."

Day 2 — Naming False Sacrifice

- Re-read the Week 10 summary
- Write a list titled: **"Things I Endured That God Never Asked Me To"**
- Reflect on what each one cost you

Day 3 — Reflection Questions & Release

- Answer all reflection questions
- Write one pattern you are ready to release

Day 4 — Love Letter From God & Your Response

- Write a love letter from God affirming your worth and boundaries
- Write your response beginning with:

"God, I receive the truth that... I release the lie that..."

Day 5 — Practicing Holy Boundaries

- Set one boundary today without over-explaining
- Journal how it felt to choose peace over performance

Day 6 — Who I Am Without Self-Destruction

- Write continuously beginning with:

"When I love from freedom instead of fear, I become..."

Day 7 — Weekly Review, Prayer, and Declaration

- Review the week's insights
- Pray for strength to remain free
- Declare aloud:

"I am unchained. I refuse to return to love that costs me my soul."

WEEK 11 — WHEN SILENCE BECOMES STRENGTH

No More Chains—She Is Free

Anchor Scripture of the Week

2 Corinthians 3:17 (NIV)

"Now the Lord is the Spirit, and where the Spirit of the Lord is, there is freedom."

Why This Scripture

This verse anchors the truth that freedom is not something you earn or explain—it is something you inhabit. This week, silence becomes evidence of freedom, not fear. Where God's Spirit resides, chains cannot remain.

Personal Story of the Week —"When Silence Stopped Begging"

There was a time when silence terrified me.

Silence meant abandonment.

Silence meant rejection.

Silence meant I had done something wrong.

So I filled it.

I explained myself.

I over-communicated.

I chased clarity from people who had already decided not to honor me.
But then something shifted.
One day, I didn't respond.
I didn't defend.
I didn't justify my needs or soften my boundaries.
And the world didn't collapse.
Instead, *I breathed*.
That was the moment I realized:
Silence wasn't punishment.
It was **power**.
I was no longer trying to earn my right to exist.
I was no longer negotiating my worth.
I was no longer bound.
Silence became my strength—
because I was finally free.

Weekly Focus

This week is about **embodied freedom**.

You are no longer breaking chains—you are walking without them.

You are learning to exist without permission.

You are discovering that silence can be a boundary, a sanctuary, and a declaration all at once.

This is the week where freedom settles into your body, not just your mind.

Optional Reading (Companion Book)

Unchained: The Awakening of the Empath's Soul — Chapter 11

When Silence Becomes Strength

Key Truth of the Week

Your silence is no longer weakness—it is wisdom.

By the End of Week 11, You Will:

- Distinguish holy sacrifice from self-betrayal
- Establish non-negotiable boundaries without guilt
- Claim silence as strength, not punishment
- Practice breathing, existing, and living without permission
- Walk confidently in freedom without explanation

Part Eleven — No More Chains

Freedom That Lives in the Body

Full Summary

The empath's freedom is born in silence.

What once felt like abandonment becomes the soil of awakening. In the quiet, the empath realizes that her breath does not belong to another person's approval. Her presence does not require validation. Her existence does not need permission.

Silence becomes the place where chains lose their sound.

This chapter guides you into embodied freedom—where self-love replaces self-abandonment, where boundaries become sacred, and where you rise not by fighting, but by *being*.

Key Takeaway

Silence is not absence—it is power. In the quiet, the empath rises free.

Reflection Questions for Week 11

After each response, write:
"This is where my freedom lives."

1. How did silence in past relationships feel like punishment or rejection?
2. What does it mean for you to breathe without permission—to exist fully without seeking validation?
3. In what ways can you consciously choose *better* over bitterness in your healing?
4. How can you redirect the love you once poured outward toward yourself?

Core Exercise 1 — Identifying Chains

Complete the table honestly:

Past Relationship / Situation
Chain I Experienced
Freedom Step I Can Take Today

Objective:
Identify lingering bondage and take tangible steps toward freedom and self-empowerment.

Core Exercise 2 — Breathing Without Permission

Instructions:
Set a timer for 5–10 minutes.
With each **inhale**, say slowly:
"I am free. I am loved. I am worthy. I am whole."
With each **exhale**, release:
fear, shame, manipulation, obligation.

Journal Prompts

- What emotions surfaced during this exercise?
- How did your body respond to slowing down and breathing intentionally?
- What does it feel like to take up space unapologetically?
- What new possibilities emerge when you honor your own breath?

Core Exercise 3 — Declaration of Freedom

Write your personal declaration of liberty. You may begin with:

- "I am free."
- "I am loved."
- "I am worthy."
- "I am whole."

Add your own language until the declaration feels *true* in your body.

Optional:

Post this declaration somewhere visible. Speak it aloud each morning this week.

Weekly Action Step

- Establish **one clear boundary** that reflects your new life
- Practice holding it **without over-explaining**
- Notice how silence changes your nervous system

At week's end, journal:

"This is how freedom feels when I don't apologize for it."

Weekly Declaration

Speak aloud daily:
"I am free.
I am loved.
I am whole.
My silence is not a cage—it is a fortress.
I do not explain my worth. I live it."

Daily Regimen for Week 11

Day 1 — Scripture & Boundaries

- Read 2 Corinthians 3:17
- Write about how boundaries were treated in your early life
- Finish:

"This is why I struggle with boundaries today…"

Day 2 — Sacrifice vs. Self-Destruction

- Re-read Week 11 concepts
- Write two paragraphs:
- One describing **holy sacrifice**
- One describing **self-destruction** in your life
- Be clear. Be honest. Be uncompromising.

Day 3 — Reflection & Lines in the Sand

- Answer all reflection questions
- Then write:

"From this day forward, I will no longer sacrifice my ______ for anyone."

Day 4 — Declaration of Liberty

- Write a bold declaration beginning with:

"I will no longer confuse sacrifice with self-neglect..."

- Read it aloud with conviction

Day 5 — Practicing a Boundary in Real Time

- Choose one boundary to practice today
- Do not explain it
- At night, journal:
- What happened
- How others reacted
- How you felt

Day 6 — Embracing Silence as Strength

- Choose silence instead of chasing clarity
- Write what surfaced: panic, peace, fear, empowerment
- Do not judge it—observe it

Day 7 — Weekly Review, Prayer, and Declaration

- Review the week
- Pray for courage to remain free
- Declare aloud:

"No more chains. My silence is strength. My boundaries are holy. My heart is protected."

Affirmation / Reflection

"No more chains.
No more cages.
No more captivity.
I breathe deeply, love fully, and walk in freedom.
My silence is my strength.
My heart is my sanctuary.
I am awakened, empowered, and unshakable."

A Prayer of Release

Father,

I lay down every chain that tried to hold me captive.

I release every voice that silenced me, every lie that told me I was unworthy.

Today, I embrace Your silence—not as abandonment, but as the womb of my awakening.

I breathe in Your love.
I exhale the pain.
I breathe in freedom.
I exhale fear.
I breathe in worth.
I exhale shame.

From this moment forward, I will love myself with the same devotion I once poured into empty places.

I will guard my heart with truth, not bitterness.
I rise—not as a victim, but as a victor.
No more chains.
No more cages.
No more captivity.
I am free.
Amen.

WEEK 12 — THE EMPATH'S CALLING

She Will Soar

Anchor Scripture of the Week

Isaiah 61:1–3 (NIV)

"The Spirit of the Sovereign Lord is on me,
because the Lord has anointed me
to proclaim good news to the poor…
to bind up the brokenhearted,
to proclaim freedom for the captives
and release from darkness for the prisoners."

Why This Scripture

This scripture seals the journey. It affirms that what you survived was not random—it was preparation. The empath's healing is not only personal; it is purposeful. God restores you so that you may restore others, not from wounds, but from overflow.

Chapter Summary

The empath's journey culminates in her calling.

From breaking to awakening, silence to exposure, she emerges whole, unchained, and empowered. What once felt like loss has become assignment. What once caused pain now births purpose.

This chapter guides you to recognize your divine design, love from abundance instead of depletion, and step confidently into your prophetic assignment. Your empathy is no longer a liability—it is a wellspring of healing, wisdom, and ministry.

Key Takeaway

What once brought pain now births purpose. Your heart is not fragile—it is a vessel for life, healing, and freedom.

Reflection Questions for Week 12

After each response, write:
"This is part of my calling."

1. How has your empathy transformed through this journey—from vulnerability to strength?
2. What areas of your life are now ready to overflow with God's love and purpose?
3. How can you love yourself while maintaining boundaries that protect your heart?
4. In what ways can your story become a ministry to others who are silent, broken, or unseen?

Core Exercise 1 — Naming Your Calling

Complete the table below:

Gift / Strength
How It Was Misused
How It Will Be Used Now

Objective:
Identify your God-given gifts, acknowledge how they were previously exploited, and declare how they will now be stewarded with wisdom,

boundaries, and purpose.

Core Exercise 2 — Prophetic Declaration

Read aloud, meditate on, and then **write your own declaration**, inspired by the statements below:

"I am whole. I am chosen. I am unshaken."

"I am a voice for the silent, light in the darkness, and love poured from the overflow of God's Spirit."

"Every chain that bound me is now evidence of my freedom. Every tear has birthed joy. Every battle has crowned me with victory."

Optional Practice:

Post your declaration somewhere visible or record it as a voice memo and listen daily.

Core Exercise 3 — Ministry of Empathy

Journal thoughtfully:

- Who around me needs the healed version of me?
- How can I serve from abundance, not emptiness?
- What boundaries must I maintain to protect my calling?

Note: This exercise is not about over-giving again. It is about **serving wisely, sustainably, and spiritually**.

Weekly Action Step

Take **one small step** into your calling this week:

- Share part of your story
- Encourage someone intentionally
- Begin outlining a ministry, group, or project

- Volunteer or mentor
- Pray for clarity and obedience

Journal:
"This is how it felt to move forward instead of shrinking back."

Weekly Declaration

Speak aloud daily:
"I am free.
I am chosen.
I am unstoppable.
My empathy is my ministry, not my downfall.
My story is a weapon against darkness.
I will soar."

Daily Regimen for Week 12

Day 1 — Scripture & Calling

- Read Isaiah 61:1–3
- Write about a moment you knew you were created for more
- Finish:

"If fear wasn't loud, God would use me to..."

Day 2 — Gifts Once Used Against You

- List your core gifts
- Write how each was misused
- Rewrite how each will now be used for good

Day 3 — Reflection Questions: Destiny Edition

- Answer all Week 12 reflection questions
- Then write:

"This is how my story can help set someone else free..."

Day 4 — Prophetic Declaration Over Your Life

- Write a declaration beginning with:

"I am whole. I am chosen. I am unshaken..."

- Include where you will go, who you will serve, and how you will live healed

Day 5 — One Step Into Purpose

- Take one tangible action toward your calling
- Journal how it felt to act instead of wait

Day 6 — Protecting Your Calling

Write two lists:

- "To protect my calling, I must say no to..."
- "To nurture my calling, I must say yes to..."

Day 7 — Final Review, Prayer, and Declaration

- Review all 12 weeks
- Write a prayer of gratitude and dedication
- Declare aloud:

"I am free. I am whole. I am loved. I am chosen.
I will not go back.
I will soar."

EPILOGUE — WALKING IN YOUR FREEDOM

Beloved Empath,

You have walked through the fire.

You have faced the pain, the silence, the exposure, and the awakening.

And here you are—

Still standing.

Still breathing.

Still loving.

But now, loving yourself first.

The chains that once bound you no longer define you.

The need for approval no longer controls you.

The lies that questioned your worth have been silenced by truth.

You are not broken.

You are not defeated.

You are strong, clear, and divinely called.

A Letter to Your Soul

Dear One,

I see you. I know the battles you fought silently. I was with you in every tear, every ache, every unanswered prayer.

Your love was not wasted. It was refining you for purpose.

Every moment of invisibility was preparation for authority.

Every season of pain was shaping you for freedom.

Now, take your next step with courage.

The past is behind you.

The lessons are within you.

The future is calling your name.

Final Invitation to Reflection

Journal quietly:

- What have I laid down?
- Who am I now that I am unchained?
- How will I guard this freedom?

Ask God:

"How can I honor my empathy and walk in my calling today?"

Closing Reflections — Walking Fully in Your Freedom

Key Takeaways

- Your empathy is a divine gift, not a burden
- Boundaries are holy and necessary
- Love flows from abundance, not fear
- Pain became awakening
- God's love defines your worth

Next Steps

- Protect your heart
- Practice self-compassion
- Journal redemption, not regret
- Stay connected to healthy community
- Use your story to heal others

Closing Affirmation

Speak aloud:

"I am free.
I am whole.
I am loved.
I am chosen.
I walk in authority, joy, and purpose."

Final Encouragement

Be grateful for every step that brought you here.
Celebrate yourself.
Your story does not end here—it **soars**.
Go forth, beloved.
Live unchained.
Love wisely.
And walk boldly into your calling.

www.ingramcontent.com/pod-product-compliance
Lightning Source LLC
Chambersburg PA
CBHW061703120626
46550CB00003B/1070

9781970671117